GOD HASN'T CHANGED HIS MIND

DR. BILL BENNETT

God Hasn't Changed His Mind
Copyright © 2012

All Rights Reserved.

No part of this book may be reproduced in any form without permission in writing from the author or publisher.

ISBN-13: 978-1-935256-15-1

Published by L'Edge Press
P.O. Box 1652
Boone, NC 28607

DEDICATION

Dedicated to my sons, Philip Judson Bennett and David Palmer Bennett who, though physically bound in wheel chairs, at the same time abound in the love of Jesus, encouraging more hearts and touching more lives than anyone I know.

FOREWORD

Assaults Upon The Ten Commandments?

Virtually all Americans and our founding fathers believed that the Ten Commandments form the basis of the moral and legal standards of the USA. But the Supreme Court of the US within the last generation has rejected this view. Consequently in 1980 in the case of <u>Stone v. Graham</u>, the court shocked the nation by striking down a Kentucky stature which required the posting privately of funded Ten Commandment displays "on the wall of each public classroom in the State." This was but the beginning of a "Search and Destroy the Ten Commandments" which continues to this hour. In fact the ACLU has asked its supporters to hunt down every display of the Ten Commandments for the purpose of eradicating them by judicial action.[1] Those who know their Old Testament will recall that when the worship of Baal became a national scandal, God raised up the prophet Elijah to "hunt down and destroy the statures of Baal" throughout God's land."[2] "Isn't it ironic in post-Christian America to find an organization mobilizing its forces to hunt down and destroy across our land one of the most prominent public symbols of the same God who showed His power against the priests of Baal in the days of Elijah?"[3] It is abundantly clear from the facts of history that the Supreme Court of the US over the years has executed a judicial coup d'etat.

The most publicized action of the court in its assaults on the Ten Commandments was that involving Chief Justice Roy Moore of Alabama. After assuming office Justice Moore who was yielding private funds, caused a 5200 pound granite monument to be

---

[1] Pat Robertson, *The Ten Offenses*, p. 51
[2] *Ibid.*
[3] *Ibid.*

carved out to display the Ten Commandments. This monument was located in a prominent spot in the rotunda of the building which houses the Supreme Court of Alabama.

The people of Alabama were strongly in support of Judge Moore's action, but the ACLU brought a suit in the Montgomery Federal District Court to have the monument removed. The US District Court ordered the monument removed. Judge Moore appealed, but did not ask for a timely stay of the order, until it appeared he was in contempt of court. Therefore, he was suspended from his post by his Alabama colleagues. On November 13, 2003, J. Moore was removed from the bench by the nine members of the Supreme Court for having "placed himself above the law."[4]

The monument was hauled away and dumped out of sight of the public in a storeroom. When asked about his action by reporters, Judge Moore replied, "I have absolutely no regrets," and to his supporters at the courthouse in Montgomery, he said, "It's about whether or not you can acknowledge God as a source of our law and our liberty."[5] Judge Moore's case reveals the absolute determination of the highest court in our land to eradicate the Ten Commandments in our land, in opposition to our founding fathers, the US Constitution, and the Constitutions of the 50 States. The irony of such action is that as the nine unelected Justices made their decision the Ten Commandments were inscribed above their heads in the Supreme Court Building in Washington, D. C. Rob Schenck, President of the National Clergy Council, declared to the courts, "If you can display these Ten Commandments above your head, why can't the people of Alabama display them in the rotunda of their Supreme Court Building?"

How far will the Supreme Court go in its efforts to eradicate religion from the public arena? Based upon its previous actions, "The State of California will be forced to change the religious names of its

---

[4] *Ibid.* p. 51
[5] *Ibid.* p. 51

three principal cities; Los Angeles (the angels), San Francisco (the Catholic Saint Francis) and Sacramento (the sacraments of the Christian church). Or should two cities named Santa Fe (holy faith) be forced by the Supreme Court to change their names for being religiously motivated. Or how about Los Cruces (the crosses) in New Mexico or the Sangre de Christo (blood of Christ) mountains, also in New Mexico? Perhaps the Court will next take aim at St. Louis, Missouri; or Zion, Illinois; or Bethlehem, Pennsylvania: or St. Paul, Minnesota; or St. Petersburg, Florida. Where could it ever end?

Frankly, we are left with the inescapable conclusion that either the majority of the Court is made up of illogical left-wing fanatics or people so trapped by their own convoluted reasoning that they don't see the emotional, political, and spiritual shipwreck they are slowly but surely bringing on this great nation.

The unelected judges have stolen power not granted them by the Constitution of the USA nor the Constitutions of all 50 States and have used it for decades to wage a relentless and all-out war against the Judeo-Christian foundation of the most wonderful nation in the history of human kind. Example: Justice Scalia, a conservative member of the Court, declared in 2003 that the Supreme Court had declared "sodomy" a constitutional right though it was a criminal offense at the time of the founding and for some 200 years thereafter.[6]

Let the Constitution of the USA and the 50 States speak their positions on God and religion:

1st of the 10 "Bill of Rights" "Congress shall make no law respecting the establishment of religion and the free exercise thereof."

---

[6] *Ibid.* p. 52

ALABAMA (1901)

Preamble: "We, the people of the State of Alabama, in order to establish justice, insure domestic tranquility, and secure the blessings of liberty to ourselves and our posterity, invoking the favor and guidance of <u>Almighty God,</u> do ordain and establish the following Constitution and form of government for the State of Alabama."

ALASKA (R. 1956 O. 1959)

"We the people of Alaska, <u>grateful to God</u> and to those who founded our nation and pioneered this great land, in order to secure and transmit to succeeding generations our heritage of political, civil and religious liberty within the Union of States, do ordain and establish this constitution for the State of Alaska."

ARIZONA (1910)

Preamble: "We the people of the State of Arizona, grateful to <u>Almighty God</u> for our liberties, do ordain this Constitution."

ARKANSAS (1874)

Preamble: "We, the people of the State of Arkansas, grateful to <u>Almighty God</u> for the privilege of choosing our own form of government, for our civil and religious liberty, and desiring to perpetuate its blessings and secure the same to our selves and posterity, do ordain and establish this Constitution."

CALIFORNIA

Preamble: "We, the People of the State of California, grateful to <u>Almighty God</u> for our freedom, in order to secure and perpetuate its blessings, do establish this Constitution."

COLORADO (1876)

Preamble: "We, the people of Colorado, with profound reverence for the <u>Supreme Ruler of the Universe</u>…do ordain and establish this constitution for the State of Colorado."

CONNECTICUT (1963)

Preamble: "The People of Connecticut acknowledging with gratitude, the good providence of God, in having permitted them to enjoy a free government; do…herby, after a careful consideration and revision, ordain and establish the following constitution and form of civil government."

DELAWARE (1897)

Preamble: "Through Divine goodness, all men have by nature the rights of worshiping and serving their Creator according to the dictates of their conscience…"

ARTICLE I.1. Freedom of religion.
Section 1. Although it is the duty of all men frequently to assemble together for the public worship of Almighty God; and piety and morality, on which the prosperity of communities depends, are hereby promoted…"

FLORIDA (1885/1968)

Preamble: "We, the people of the State of Florida, being grateful to Almighty God for our constitutional liberty, in order to secure its benefits, perfect our government, insure domestic tranquility, maintain public order, and guarantee equal civil and political rights to all, do ordain and establish this constitution."

GEORGIA (1777/1985)

Preamble: "To perpetuate the principles of free government, insure justice to all, preserve peace, promote the interest and happiness of the citizen and of the family, and transmit to posterity the enjoyment of liberty, we the people of Georgia, relying upon the protection and guidance of Almighty God, do ordain and establish this Constitution."

ARTICLE I. SECTION 1. RIGHTS OF PERSONS
Paragraph III. Freedom of conscience: Each person has the natural and inalienable right to worship God, each according to the Dictates

of the person's own conscience; and no human authority should, in any case, Control or interfere with such rights of conscience.

HAWAII

Preamble: "We, the people of Hawaii, grateful for <u>Divine Guidance</u>, and mindful of our Hawaiian heritage and uniqueness as an island State, do hereby ordain and establish this constitution for the State of Hawaii."

IDAHO (1890)

Preamble: "We, the people of the state of Idaho, grateful to <u>Almighty God</u> for our freedom, to secure its blessings and promote our common welfare do establish this Constitution."

ARTICLE 1. SECTION 4. GUARANTY OF RELIGIOUS LIBERTY.
"The exercise and enjoyment of religious faith and worship shall forever be guaranteed; and no person shall be denied any civil or political right, privilege, or capacity on account of his religious opinions."

ILLINOIS (1970)

Preamble; We, the People of the State of Illinois—grateful to <u>Almighty God</u> for the civil, political and religious liberty which He has permitted us to enjoy and seeking His blessing upon our endeavors…do ordain and establish this constitution for the State of Illinois."

INDIANA (1970)

Preamble: "To the end, that justice be established, public order maintained, and liberty perpetuated: WE, the People of the State of Indiana, grateful to <u>ALMIGHTY GOD</u> for the free exercise of the right to choose our own form of government, do ordain this Constitution."

ARTICLE 1.S1: "We declare, that all people are created equal; that they are endowed by their CREATOR with certain inalienable rights"

ARTICLE 1. SECTION 2. RIGHT TO WORSHIP
"All people shall be secured in the natural right to worship ALMIGHTY GOD, according to the dictates of their own consciences."

IOWA
Preamble: "We the people of the state of Iowa, grateful to the Supreme Being for the blessings hitherto enjoyed, and feeling our dependence on Him for a continuation of those blessings, do ordain and establish a free and independent government by the name of the State of Iowa…"

KANSAS
Preamble: "We, the people of Kansas, grateful to Almighty God for our civil and religious privileges, in order to insure the full enjoyment of our rights as American citizens, do ordain and establish this constitution of the state of Kansas."

Religious liberty. "The right to worship God according to the dictates of conscience shall never be infringed."

KENTUCKY (1792/1891)
Preamble: "We, the people of the Commonwealth of Kentucky, grateful to Almighty God for the civil, political and religious liberties we enjoy, and invoking the continuance of these blessings, do ordain and establish this Constitution."

Section 1: "All men are, by nature, free and equal, and have certain inherent and inalienable rights, among which may be reckoned… Second: The right of worshipping Almighty God according to the dictates of their consciences."

LOUISIANA (1974)

Preamble: "We, the people of Louisiana, grateful to <u>Almighty God</u> for the civil, political, economic, and religious liberty we enjoy… do ordain and establish this constitution."

MAINE

Preamble: "We the people of Maine,…acknowledging with grateful hearts the goodness of the <u>Sovereign Ruler</u> of the Universe in affording us an opportunity, so favorable to the design; and, imploring God's aid and direction in its accomplishment, do agree to form ourselves into a free and independent State, by the style and title of the State of Maine and do ordain and establish the following Constitution for the government of the same."

Section 3. "All individuals have a natural and unalienable right to worship <u>Almighty God</u> according to the dictates of their own consciences, and no person shall be hurt, molested or restrained in that person's liberty or estate for worshipping God in the manner and season most agreeable to the dictates of that person's own conscience."

MARYLAND (1867/2002)

Preamble: "We, the People of the State of Maryland, grateful to <u>Almighty God</u> for our civil and religious liberty, and taking into our serious consideration the best means of establishing a good Constitution in this State for the sure foundation and more permanent security thereof, declare…"

Art. 36 "That as it is the duty of every man to worship <u>God</u> in such a manner as he thinks most acceptable to Him…"

Art. 37 "That no religious test ought ever to be required as a qualification for any office of profit or trust in this State, other than a declaration of the belief in the existence of <u>God</u>."

Art. 39 "That the manner of administering an oath or affirmation to any person, ought to be such as those of the religious persuasion, profession, or denomination, of which he is a member, generally esteem, the most effectual confirmation by the attestation of the <u>Divine Being</u>."

MASSACHUSETTS

Preamble: "I…We, therefore, the people of Massachusetts, acknowledging, with grateful hearts, the goodness of the <u>great Legislator</u> of the universe, in affording us, in the course of His providence, an opportunity, deliberately and peaceably, without fraud, violence or surprise, of entering into an original, explicit, and solemn compact with each other; and of forming a new constitution of civil government, for ourselves and posterity; and devoutly imploring His direction in so interesting a design, do agree upon, ordain and establish the following Declaration or Rights, and Frame of Government, as the Constitution of the Commonwealth of Massachusetts."

Article II. "It is the right as well as the duty of all men in society, publicly, and at stated seasons to worship the Supreme Being, the great Creator and Preserver of the universe. And no subject shall be hurt, molested, or restrained, in his person, liberty, or estate, for worshipping God in the manner and season most agreeable to the dictates of his own conscience; or for his religious profession or sentiments; provided he doth not disturb the public peach, or obstruct others in their religious worship."

MICHIGAN

Preamble: "We the people of the State of Michigan, grateful to <u>Almighty God</u> for the blessings of freedom, and earnestly desiring to secure these blessings undiminished, to ourselves and our posterity, do ordain, and establish this constitution."

ARTICLE.E I, Sec.4: "Every person shall be at liberty to worship <u>God</u> according to the dictates of his own conscience."

MINNESOTA (1897/1998)

Preamble: "We, the people of the state of Minnesota, <u>grateful to God</u> for our civil and religious liberty, and desiring to perpetuate its blessings and secure the same to ourselves and our posterity, do ordain and establish this Constitution."

MISSISSIPPI (1890)

Preamble: "We, the people of Mississippi in convention assemble, <u>grateful to Almighty God</u> and involving his blessing on our work, do ordain and establish this Constitution."

ARTICLE 3. Sec.18. "No religious test as a qualification for office shall be required; and no preference shall be given by law to any religious sect or mode of worship: but the free enjoyment of all religious sentiments and the different modes of worship shall be held sacred. The rights hereby secured shall not be construed to justify acts of licentiousness injurious to morals or dangerous to the peace and safety of the state, or to exclude the Holy Bible from use in any public school of this state."

MISSOURI

Preamble: "We the people of Missouri, with profound reverence for the <u>Supreme Ruler</u> of the Universe, and grateful for His goodness, do establish this constitution for the better government of the state."

ARTICLE 1, sec. 5 "That all men have a natural and indefeasible right to worship <u>Almighty God</u> according to the dictates of their own consciences."

MONTANA

Preamble: "We the people of Montana, <u>grateful to God</u> for the quiet beauty of our state, the grandeur of our mountains, the vastness of our rolling plains, and desiring to improve the quality of life, equality of opportunity and to secure the blessings of liberty for this and future generations do ordain and establish this constitution."

NEBRASKA

Preamble: "We, the people, grateful to <u>Almighty God</u> for our freedom, do ordain and establish the following declaration of rights and frame of government, as the Constitution of the State of Nebraska."

ARTICLE 1. Sec 4 "All persons have a natural and indefeasible right to worship <u>Almighty God</u> according to the dictates of their own consciences."

NEVADA

Preamble: "We the people of the State of Nevada, Grateful to <u>Almighty God</u> for our freedom in order to secure its blessings, insure domestic tranquility, and form a more perfect Government, do establish this Constitution."

NEW HAMPSHIRE (1784/1990)

(Art.)5. (Religious Freedom Recognized) "Every individual has a natural and unalienable right to worship <u>God</u> according to the dictates of his own conscience, and reason."

NEW JERSEY (1947)

Preamble: "We, the people of the State of New Jersey, grateful to <u>Almighty God</u> for the civil and religious liberty which He hath so long permitted us to enjoy, and looking to Him for a blessing upon our endeavors to secure and transmit the same unimpaired to succeeding generations, do ordain and establish this Constitution."

NEW MEXICO (1911/1974)

Preamble: "We, the people of New Mexico, grateful to <u>Almighty God</u> for the blessings of Liberty, in order to secure the advantage of a state government, do ordain and establish this Constitution."

NEW YORK (1938/2002)

Preamble: "We, The People of the State of New York, <u>grateful to Almighty God</u> for our Freedom, in order to secure its blessings, do establish this constitution."

NORTH CAROLINA

Preamble: "We. The people of the State of North Carolina, grateful to <u>Almighty God</u>, the Sovereign Ruler of Nations, for the preservation of the American Union and the existence of our civil, political, and religious liberties, and acknowledging our dependence upon Him for the continuance of those blessings to s and our posterity, do, for the more certain security thereof and for the better government of this State, ordain and establish Constitution."

ARTICLE 1. Sec. 13. "All persons have a natural and inalienable right to worship Almighty God according to the dictates of their own consciences, and no human authority shall, in any case whatever, control or interfere with the rights of conscience."

NORTH DAKOTA

Preamble: "We the people of North Dakota, grateful to <u>Almighty God</u> for the blessings of civil and religious liberty, do ordain and establish this constitution."

Section 3. "The free exercise and enjoyment of religious profession and worship, without discrimination or preference shall be forever guaranteed in this state."

OHIO

Preamble: "We, the people of the State of Ohio, grateful to <u>Almighty God</u> for our freedom to secure its blessings and promote our common welfare, do establish this Constitution."

Section 1.07 "Rights of conscience; education; the necessity of religion and knowledge (1851) All men have a natural and indefeasible right to worship <u>Almighty God</u> according to the dictates of their own conscience....Religion, morality, and knowledge, however, being essential to good government, it shall be the duty of the general assembly to pass suitable laws to protect every religious denomination in the peaceable enjoyment of its own mode of public worship, and to encourage schools and the means of instruction."

OKLAHOMA (1907/1975)

Article: I. Sec. 2 "Perfect toleration of religious sentiment shall be secured, and no inhabitant of the State shall ever be molested in person or property on account of his or her mode of religious worship."

OREGON (1857/1859)

Article 1, Section 2. "All men shall be secure in the Natural right, to worship Almighty God according to the dictates of their own consciences."

PENNSYLVANIA

Preamble: "We, the people of the Commonwealth of Pennsylvania, grateful to Almighty God for the blessings of civil and religious liberty, and humbly invoking His guidance, do ordain and establish this constitution."

ARTICLE I. Sec. 3 "All men have a natural and indefeasible right to worship Almighty God according to the dictates of their own consciences."

ARTICLE 1. Sec. 4 "No person who acknowledges the being of a God and a future state of rewards and punishments shall, on account of his religious sentiments, be disqualified to hold any office or place of trust or profit under this Commonwealth."

RHODE ISLAND (1843)

Preamble: "We, the people of the State of Rhode Island and Providence Plantations, grateful to Almighty God for the civil and religious liberty which He hath so long permitted us to enjoy, and looking to Him for a blessing upon our endeavors to secure and to transmit the same, unimpaired, to succeeding generations, do ordain and establish this Constitution of government."

ARTICLE I. Sec. 3 "Whereas <u>Almighty God</u> hath created the mind free; and all the attempts to influence it by temporal punishments or burdens, or by civil incapacitations, tend to beget habits of hypocrisy and meanness; and whereas a principal object of our venerable ancestors, in their migration to this country and their settlement of this state, was, as they expressed it, to hold forth a lively experiment that a flourishing civil state may stand and be best maintained with full liberty in religious concernment;…"

SOUTH CAROLINA

Sec. 2. "The General Assembly shall make no law respecting an establishment of religion or prohibiting the free exercise thereof, or abridging the freedom of speech or of the press or the right of the people to peaceably to assemble and petition the government or any department thereof for a redress of grievances."

SOUTH DAKOTA

Preamble: "We, the people of South Dakota, <u>grateful to Almighty God</u> for our civil and religious liberties…do ordain and establish the Constitution for the State of South Dakota."

ARTICLE 6. Sec.3. "The right to worship <u>God</u> according to the dictates of conscience shall never be infringed."

TENNESSEE

ARTICLE I. Sec. 3 "That all men have a natural and indefeasible right to worship <u>Almighty God</u> according to the dictates of their own conscience…"

TEXAS

Preamble: "humbly invoking the blessings of <u>Almighty God</u>, the people of the Stat of Texas, do ordain and establish this Constitution."

UTAH

Preamble: Grateful to <u>Almighty God</u> for life and liberty, we, the people of Utah, in order to secure and perpetuate the principles of free government , do ordain and establish this Constitution."

VERMONT (1793)

ARTICLE 3. "That all persons have a natural and unalienable right to worship <u>Almighty God</u>, according to the dictates of their own consciences and understandings, as in their opinion shall be regulated by the word of God."

VIRGINIA

ARTICLE 1.Sec. 16. "That religion or the duty which we owe our <u>Creator</u>, and the manner of discharging it, can be directed only by reason and conviction, not by force or violence, and, therefore, all men are equally entitled to the free exercise of religion, according to the dictate of conscience; and that it is the mutual duty of all to practice Christian forbearance, love, and charity to each other."

WASHINGTON

Preamble: We, the people of the State of Washington, grateful to the <u>Supreme Ruler of the Universe</u> for tour liberties, do ordain this constitution."

WEST VIRGINIA

Preamble: "Since through <u>Divine Providence</u> we enjoy the blessings of civil, political and religious liberty, we, the people of West Virginia, in and through the provisions of this Constitution, reaffirm our faith in and constant reliance upon god and seek diligently to promote, preserve and perpetuate good government in the state of West Virginia for the common welfare, freedom and security of ourselves and our posterity."

WISCONSIN

Preamble: "We the people of Wisconsin, grateful to <u>Almighty God</u> for our freedom, in order to secure its blessings, form a more perfect government, insure domestic tranquility and promote the general welfare, do establish this constitution."

WYOMING

Preamble: "We, the people of the State of Wyoming, <u>grateful to God</u> for our civil, political and religious liberties, and desiring to secure them to ourselves and perpetuate them to our posterity, do ordain this Constitution" [7]

---

[7] *Ibid.* pp. 209-219.

INTRODUCTION

I am deeply troubled that the unelected Supreme Court of only nine men is seeking to remove the Ten Commandments from the public square and thus from the lives of millions of Americans who cherish them as the moral law of the land and also the moral standards of our citizens. For this reason I have written this little volume in which I endeavor to accomplish three objectives:

1. to expound the meaning of each commandment.
2. to explain how each commandment applies to the lives of Christians in the new millennium.
3. to exhort Christians to obey the Ten Commandments today through the power of agape love.
4. to exhort preachers to preach more on the Ten Commandments.
5. to encourage God's people to incorporate the Ten Commandments in their daily lives.

It is my prayer that the Holy Spirit will use this book to accomplish these five purposes "to the praise of the glory of His grace." Soli Deo Gloria.

Bill Bennett

TABLE OF CONTENTS

Chapter One:
Let God Be God 1

Chapter Two:
The God Who Can Tolerate No Rivals 7

Chapter Three:
God's Last Name is not Dammit 11

Chapter Four:
The Sabbath – Holy Day or Holiday 15

Chapter Five:
Don't Forget Dear Ole Mom and Dad 19

Chapter Six:
Tampering with God's Most Sacred Gift 25

Chapter Seven:
It's Sex O'Clock in America 29

Chapter Eight:
Why There is no Free Lunch 35

Chapter Nine:
Hung by the Tongue 39

Chapter Ten:
A "Respectable" But Devastating Sin 45

Chapter Eleven:
Can A Christian Keep the Ten Commandments? 51

1
LET GOD BE GOD
"You Shall Have No Other Gods Before Me"
Exodus 20:3

Let us seek to delve into the profound meaning and application of this first commandment under the following four headings:

I. THE AUTHORITY OF THIS COMMANDMENT - Before speaking this commandment, God said, "I am Jehovah the God," meaning "I am He who was, who is, and is to come." Thus, the God who speaks the 10 Commandments is the ever-present, ever active, all powerful, all righteous, creator and redeemer of humankind.

A. Note Two Definitions:
 1. God – Anything, worthy or unworthy, to which any individual gives his or her ultimate affection, time, energy, and devotion. Martin Luther said, "That upon which you set your heart and put your trust is probably your God."
 2. 10 Commandments – God's timeless moral law for today's lawless world.
B. Unchanging – Human rules change, but God's law never changes.
C. Irrepealably – Impossible to be withdrawn or revoked.
D. Universal – The 10 Commandments are universal which means they are not just for Hebrews, but for all humankind and all ages.

II. ANALYSIS OF THE FIRST COMMANDMENT
A. Negative:
 1. It is not a commandment against <u>atheism</u> – The intelligence of man will not embrace atheism. Ecclesiastes 3:11a says, "He (God) hath made every thing beautiful in his time; also

he hath set the world in their heart, so that no man can find out the work that God maketh from the beginning to the end."

    2. It is not a COMMANDMENT TO WORSHIP GOD – Human beings instinctively worship some God. The tragedy is, this instinct for God can be diverted toward the wrong kind of God.

B. Positive:
    1. There is ONE and only one true God. There is no place for polytheism, pantheism, or henotheism, but only monotheism because there is only one true God.

    2. The only true God is Jehovah God of the Old Testament.

    3. The true God is fully revealed in Jesus of Nazareth. In John 14:9b, Jesus said, "…he that hath seen me hath seen the Father…"

    4. He is the true God and He alone is to be worshipped. Jesus said in Matthew 4:10b,"…for it is written, Thou shalt worship the Lord thy God, and Him only shalt thy serve."

III. APPLICATION OF FIRST COMMANDMENT TO LIFE: TODAY'S SURROGATE GODS: The tragedy today is that so many of us, like people in the book of Kings, claim to serve the Lord but really serve other gods. Modern man has shaped a pantheon of false gods. They're so subtle, so clever, so taken for granted as a part of everyday like that it is difficult to keep them off God's solitary throne in our hearts. You and I may laugh at the heathen bowing before a grotesque idol, but be totally unaware that the sophisticated substitute that we have put in God's place is just as grotesque. Our god may be even more spiritually destructive than the idol in that Stone Age village. Let's look briefly at some of the false gods that strive to usurp the place of the true God.

These surrogate gods determine our practical everyday choices and our moral standards. Space prohibits enumerating all of the false gods abroad in our world today. However, we can look at a few to illustrate that most of our idols result from taking some good gift that God has given us, misusing that gift and making it the god of our lives.

1. SEX – (OLD NAMES, VENUS AND BAAL) This great god called "Sex" leers at us from advertisements and wiggles at us from television screens, and most modern novels and movies are simple invitations to become "Peeping Toms." Hail the great goddess, Sex. Hollywood is its prophet, and the sordid stories of its starts are its sacred scriptures.

   When we use one of God's precious gifts, like sex, as God commands and do not abuse it by making it central in our lives, it will bring ecstasy and great joy. But when we take a gift from God, forget the Giver and live for it, it will eventually let us down and even destroy us.

2. SCIENCE – Education has become an end in itself. Science has become a god. We've pinned our hopes on it for years. And now the very technology and education which were supposed to lift us to some kind of heaven by our own atomic bootstraps, and make the world a paradise with food, shelter, heat and light for all, has turned into a Frankenstein-like monster.

3. SILVER AND GOLD – (OLD NAME MAMMON) Jesus said in Luke 12:15, "…Take heed and beware of covetousness; for a man's life consisteth not in the abundance of the things which he possesseth."

4. SPORTS (PLEASURE) – OLD NAME EROS) – This also includes hobbies, television, food, etc.

5. SPIRITS – LIQUOR – (OLD NAME BACCHUS) - Alcohol and all forms of drugs are the norm in our culture today.

6. STATE –(OLD NAME MARS AND MERCURY)- Some people put their love for their country above God or as a substitute for God.

7. SELF – (OLD NAME NARCISSUS) – The greatest god of all is the god of self. This is America's foremost god which you can see expressed in Secular Humanism, the New Age Movement, Self-Help, etc.

IV. APPROPRIATION OF THE FIRST COMMANDMENT
Warning: Not many Americans would say that they are worshiping a false god, but the great danger is to permit anything in your life which rules out the true God. II Kings 17:33 says the Israelites "feared the Lord but served their own gods." This is the great sin of America today, the very sin warned against in the first commandment. Loyalty to anything less than the true God is disloyalty to the true God Himself (Matthew 6:24).

OBEDIENCE TO THE FIRST COMMANDMENT:
You must love the Lord your God with all your heart, soul, mind, and strength (Matt.22:37). To do so, you must be a Christian. For if God is loved, His Son must be received as Savior and Lord –His Son who loved and died for you on the cross.

Dr. Gallup says 95% of Americans believe in God, yet most Americans do not deny God, but simply ignore Him or consign Him to a place of meaninglessness in their lives.

Some years ago in a Scottish town, someone placed an unusual advertisement in the local newspaper. On the front page of the newspaper, a conspicuously placed notice asked the reader to look on the back page.

When the reader turned to the back page, it was empty. But those who looked closely saw, in the lower right hand corner in small print, these words:

"IS THIS WHERE YOU ARE PUTTING GOD?"

2
THE GOD WHO CAN TOLERATE NO RIVALS
"You Shall Not Make For Yourself An Idol (Image) In The Form Of Anything In Heaven Above Or On The Earth Beneath Or In The Water Below...For I, The Lord Your God, Am A Jealous God..."
(Exodus 20:4-6)

The second commandment is by no means a repetition of the first. The first commandment forbids us to have other gods beside the only true God. The second commandment tells us that we are not to create any image of the true God and bow down and worship it. The first commandment tells us WHO must be worshipped; the second tells us HOW He must be worshipped. The first forbids all false gods; the second forbids all false worship.

I. THE SUBSTANCE OF THE SECOND COMMANDMENT:
A. The second commandment does not forbid the making of all images, paintings and pictures. We know this because after giving this commandment, God commanded the Israelites to adorn the tabernacle with many images.

B. The essence of the second commandment: Man is not to make any image after heavenly or earthly pattern and bow down before it in worship. The commandment forbids us setting any image between us and God. Some say, "Images are a great help to me. They help me fix my thoughts on God. I do not worship them, but the God behind them." This is exactly what is forbidden in the commandment.

C. Practical Obedience: The best way for us to have communion with God is to close our eyes to everything that can be seen with the natural eye and open the eyes of our spirit toward our heavenly Father.

II. THE SUBTLETIES OF USING IMAGES: Images may appear to be harmless, but if used in worship they tend to degrade progressively one's concept of God, and this false concept of God will make the worshipper himself false.

PERTINENT FACTS TO PONDER:

A. A person who knows God personally through the new birth of the Holy Spirit needs no "crutch" or idol to worship God who is real in his soul. In John 4:24, Jesus says, "God is a spirit, and they who worship Him must worship Him in spirit and in truth."

B. An image of God degrades our conception of Him. This makes Him a material object when He is Spirit, holy, and faultless in every divine perfection.

C. The image ceases to be a means of worship and becomes the object of worship.

Conclusion to these points: There is a reflex influence from the image upon The worshipper. In plain words, a person becomes like the object he worships. In Psalm 115:8, we read in The Living Bible, "They that make (and worship) idols are like them…" In other words, they that make and worship idols are just as false as their idols.

III. SAMPLES OF TWENTIETH CENTURY IDOLS:

A. Obvious Idols – Some idols are obvious, such as the material means of our lives –clothes, homes, money and cars. Although they are meant to be servants, they can become idols. St. Augustine said, "Idolatry is worshipping anything that ought to be used or using anything that ought to be worshipped."

B. Not So Obvious Idols –Knowledge and wisdom can be worshipped. Sex, one of God's great gifts, can become an all-consuming passion and be worshipped. Or we may worship our government, family, children, political party, denomination, etc. The list is endless. These things are meant to be servants, but when they become and end in themselves, we become their servants and they become our gods.

C. Christian Idols –Christians are not immune to the temptation of idol worship. Note John's final words to the Ephesian Christians in 1 John 5:21, "Little children, keep yourselves from idols. Amen." Listed below are some examples of "Christian Idols"

- Idols of Men – I know some Protestants who have made idols of their pastor. I know some Roman Catholics who have made idols of their priest. The great expositor G. Campbell Morgan said, "Wherever a man gives his soul away to the priest (pastor), because he imagines that he is getting to know God through the priest (pastor), the latter becomes to the man as an image and an idol."[8]
- Idols of a denomination.
- Idols of a church building.
- Idols of forms of worship.
- Idols of the means of grace (Baptism and the Lord's Supper)
- Idols of the place called the altar.
- Idols of Doctrines – I know people to whom the doctrines of holiness, immersion baptism, and eternal security have become idols. The gift of tongues or other experiences can become idolatrous, assuming a disproportionate role in our lives.
- Idols of Self – A good argument could be made that the second commandment is the one most frequently broken today: "Thou shalt not make unto thee any graven image." You may have heard the story of two servicemen who returned to base

---

[8] G. Campbell Morgan, *The Ten Commandments*, Fleming H. Revell Company, New York, 1901, p. 30.

one Saturday night after a week's leave. They had lived it up wildly during the week and had done everything a serviceman could do on leave. On Sunday morning they went to chapel to find the chaplain preaching on the Ten Commandments. As they were slinking out the door after service, one was heard to say to the other, "Well, at least I ain't made no graven images lately!" But the problem with all that he had done, basically, was involved with the fact that he started with a graven image —not made of wood or stone, but conjured in the factory of his mind! Men create gods in their own image.

IV. SOLUTION FOR KEEPING THE SECOND COMMANDMENT:
Christ alone is the only true image of God. So says Paul in Col.1:15. He alone is worthy of our total commitment and worship. Everything else, anything else, however fine or religious, we are forbidden to worship. Why? Because we do not see the Father until we see Jesus. We cannot worship Christ until we know Him personally. Christ bids us to invite Him into our lives so we might know Him personally, and be able to worship Him in spirit and in truth (John 4:23). When we do, Paul says we are constantly being transformed into His very image by the Holy Spirit who indwells us (2 Corinthians 3:18).

3
GOD'S LAST NAME IS NOT DAMMIT
"Thou Shalt Not Take The Name Of The Lord Thy God In Vain…" (Exodus 20:7)

In an airport restroom, amid the crude graffiti that one finds on the walls in such places, someone had scrawled this line: "GOD'S LAST NAME IS NOT DAMMIT." These crude words focus on our need to heed the third commandment. Many children think God's last name is "Dammit" because that is the only way they ever hear His name mentioned in their homes.

I. THE SUBSTANCE OF THE THIRD COMMANDMENT: The concern of this commandment is that we reverence the NAME of God. We should reverence His Name simply because His Name is His very essence, His character, and His person. The Jews revered the name Yahweh (Jehovah) so much that they would not even pronounce it, lest they profaned it (they substituted Adonai or Lord). Modern names are personal labels to distinguish us from someone else, but Biblical names are descriptive of one's character.

Some Biblical examples are:
a. Jacob – Deceiver -Genesis 27:36
b. Jesus – Savior -Matthew 1:21

Thus in the New Testament you are saved, healed, your prayers are answered by the Name of Jesus. In the Old Testament God reveals both His character and actions by His Name:
a. Jehovah Raah– Genesis 16:13 – the God who sees
b. Jehovah Jireh – Genesis 22:14 – God Provides
c. Jehovah Rophe – Exodus 15:26 – the God who heals
d. Jehovah Shalom – Judges 6:24 – God my peace
e. Jehovah Roi – Psalm 23:1 – My Shepherd

f. Jehovah M'Kaddesh – Exodus 31:13 – the God who makes and keeps you holy
g. Jehovah Tsidkenu – Jeremiah 23:6 – God my righteousness
h. Jehovah Shammah – Ezekiel 48:35 – the God who is there

Therefore, to misuse, to abuse, to misapply God's Name is to denigrate, even to blaspheme, His holy character and noble actions toward men. To use His name with understanding and reverence is to glorify His name. In Matthew 6:9, Jesus restated the third commandment positively, "Our Father, Hallowed be your Name."

II. SAMPLES OF VIOLATIONS OF THE THIRD COMMANDMENT

1. PROFANITY – Some people think their vocabulary is not quite complete unless it is "enriched" by swear words. All kinds of maniacs are running around; one of the most common is the "swearomaniac."
   a. An expression used with terrible frequency is "God Damn You." God is not in the business of damning souls but of saving them. He will not satisfy your passion for revenge. When you ask Him to do so, you are insulting His holy nature and bringing great guilt upon your soul.
   b. A second frequently used expression is "Go to Hell." Why would anyone want another human being to go to this horrible place?

2. SLANGUAGE (Slang) - Some 4 letter slang words cast a shadow on God's Name:
   a. Gosh – slang for God.
   b. Heck – slang for Hell. "Hot as Hell, "Running like Hell." One man once said to me, "Preacher, that was a "Helluva Sermon."
   c. Darn – slang for Damn.
   Sadly, many Christians use these words without even realizing what they are doing or saying.

3. FRIVOLITY – Simply put, it is the using of the Lord's name in jokes, and the frivolous name of Jesus in songs. It is also attributing foolish things to God, or using degrading titles such as "The Man Upstairs," "A Living Doll," "Big Daddy," "Junior," and "Spooks"(the hippy name for the Trinity).

4. FALSE VOWS
   a. False Promises to God. An example of this would be an insincere profession of faith, baptism or the commitment to tithe and not following through.
   b. False Promises to Fellow Man. Americans used to seal agreements with a handshake- no signature or contract was required. In today's world, you have to read the fine print of the contract to be sure that they don't give to you in the big print and take away in the fine print. In Ecclesiastes 5:4, we read, "When thou soweth a vow unto God, defer not to pay it; for he hath no pleasure in fools; pay that which thou hast vowed."

5. HYPOCRISY – Some examples are as follows:
   a. G. Campbell Morgan says, "The form in which this third commandment is broken most completely, most awfully, most terribly, is by perpetually making use of the name of the Lord, while the life does not square with the profession that is made"[9]
   b. Billy Graham says, "We take the Name of God in vain when we accept it and allow ourselves to be called Christians and do not live godly lives."
   c. The Apostle Paul says, "Let every person that nameth the name of Christ depart from iniquity" (2 Timothy 2:19).
   d. Gandhi said, "I would have become a Christian if I had not met some Christians."

---

[9] G Campbell Morgan, *The Ten Commandments,* Fleming H. Revel Company, New York, 1901, p. 42.

    e. A noted Jewish Rabbi said, "We Jews have denied Jesus with our mouth; you Christians have denied Him by your lives."
    f. The person who says, "Lord, Lord" but does not obey Christ's Command (Luke 6:46).
    g. The person who sings, "All to Jesus I surrender" and surrenders nothing.
    h. The person who sings, "Take my silver and my gold, not a mite would I withhold" and won't even tithe.
    i. The person who stands as a leader but shows in his own life that he is spiritually dead and blind.

II. THE SOLUTION FOR "KEEPING" THE THIRD COMMANDMENT – One who violates this commandment has an "inside" problem and requires an "inside' job to be done on him. "Out of the heart proceed evil thoughts, murders, adulteries, fornications, thefts, false witness, blasphemies" (Matthew 15:19). If the lips are to be cleansed, the heart must be washed. If the speech is to be purified, the nature must be redeemed. The only way you can keep this commandment is to turn your life over to Jesus. "…The blood of Jesus Christ, His Son, cleanseth us from all sin" (1 John 1:7). "If any person be in Christ, He is a new creation…"(2 Cor. 5:17).

When you invite Christ to take control of your life, you will love Him and honor Him. Instead of misusing His Name, you will say, "Our Father who art in heaven, HALLOWED BE THY NAME."

4
THE SABBATH – HOLY DAY OR HOLIDAY?
"Remember The Sabbath Day To Keep It Holy."
Exodus 20:8

The first commandment instructs us to worship the true God and no other. The second commandment warns us not to create any image as an aid to worship. The third commandment warns us not to take God's name in vain. The fourth commandment sets forth a special day that God has set aside for us to worship Him. To understand the meaning of the fourth commandment, we must explore five facets of truth:

I. THE SABBATH WAS INSTITUTED BY GOD THE FATHER IN THE ORIGINAL CREATION.
This was at least 2500 years before God gave Moses the Ten Commandments. Genesis 2:2 declares, "And on the seventh day God ended His work which He had made; and He rested on the seventh day from all His work which He had done." Knowing the limitations of humankind, God in His great mercy gave us "the Sabbath" for our own good. Tallmadge, the great Presbyterian preacher, said, "Our bodies are seven-day clocks and need to be wound up. If they are not wound up, they run down into the grave. No man can continually break the Sabbath and keep his physical and mental health."

II. THE SEVENTH DAY SABBATH WAS DISCARDED FOLLOWING THE RESURRECTON OF CHRIST ON THE FIRST DAY TO ACCORD WITH THE NEW CREATION.
In its original form, THE FOURTH COMMANDMENT forbade the Hebrews to work and prescribed worship and rest on the seventh day or Saturday. Saturday was the day on which God finished the original creation (Genesis 2:2). However, Christ inaugurated the New Creation on Sunday with His resurrection from the dead. The

early Christians for a time worshipped on Saturday and Sunday, but soon began to take the Day of Christ's resurrection as their day to rest and worship (Acts 20:7; 1 Corinthians 16:2; Revelation 1:10). Our Sunday, the first day of the week, is not the same day as Saturday, the seventh day. In our Christian vocabulary of hymns and poems, we can use the word "Sabbath" as a valid figure of speech when referring to Sunday. But we should understand the two are not the same.

Note four supporting facts:
1. The fourth commandment is the only commandment that is not repeated anywhere in the New Testament.
2. The first Church Council did not require Gentile Christians to keep the Sabbath (Acts 15:19-31).
3. There is no record of Jesus or any apostle telling anyone to keep the Saturday Sabbath.
4. In all of the New Testament lists of sin, Sabbath-breaking is never mentioned.

III. THE "SABBATH DAY PRINICPLE" SHOULD BE HONORED. EVEN THOUGH THE SEVENTH DAY SABBATH HAS CEASED.

Though the letter of the Law, the seventh day Sabbath, is not applicable to us today, certainly the "Principle of the Sabbath" still is. The "Sabbath Principle" is that every human needs one day of rest and worship after six days of labor. We should observe a Sabbath day, but not necessarily Saturday. The Day of Atonement in the Old Testament was called a Sabbath, though it fell on the tenth day of the seventh month. So the word "Sabbath" is not restricted to the seventh day. Christians of the New Testament soon discarded the Saturday Sabbath, but obeyed the "Sabbath Day Principle" by keeping the first day of the week because of the Lord's resurrection. In fact they called the first day of the week "The Lord's Day" (Revelation 1:10) which for Christians is a far more appropriate name than "The Sabbath."

SABBATH VIOLATIONS HAVE REGRETTABLY CHANGED THE SABBATH FROM A HOLY DAY TO A HOLIDAY. Throughout history the observance of the Sabbath has inspired two extremes:

A. Some have made Sunday a day of gloom and depression instead of a day of joy and gladness. The Pharisees discovered 1,521 ways the Sabbath could be broken. For example, if a person was bitten by a flea, he had to permit the flea to keep on biting. If he tried to catch the flea, he would be guilty of the sin of hunting on the Sabbath. Another example was the Puritans who said that whittling must not be done on the Sabbath.

B. Our problem today is usually the opposite extreme. We have taken this day and turned it into a holiday. Some of us have taken ,to the extreme, the words of Jesus in Luke 14:5 when He said that if the ox falls in the ditch on the Sabbath, it's all right to pull it out. Sadly, we have turned it into a lot of bull. Too many put the ox into the ditch during the week so they can pull him out on Sunday. If your ox has the habit of falling into the same ditch every Sunday, it is time you either fill up the ditch or get rid of the ox.

Multitudes are sacrificing Sunday upon the altar of the twin gods of profit and pleasure.

V. THE SOLUTION FOR SABBATH VIOLATIONS IS TO MAKE JESUS CHRIST THE LORD OF YOUR LIFE.
"So the Son of Man is Lord even of the Sabbath" (Mark 2:29). So He is and when He is your Savior and Lord you will love to remember His day by keeping it holy. The true Sabbath is not only a day of rest, but also a day of worship. True worship is the highest rest of all. Cessation from work rests the body, while worship rests the spirit and the soul.

One ancient Christian creed says, the only works we should do on Sunday are "works of mercy and necessity." This is still a good guideline to follow. With the aid of the Bible and the Holy Spirit, each Christian should interpret what this means in his own life. Above all, we must not judge our fellow Christians if they do not agree with us in some details of Sabbath observances. "Let no man therefore judge you in meat, or in drink, or in respect of a holy day, or of the new moon, or of the Sabbath days" (Colossians 2:16).

In closing, let me stress that Jesus Christ is the Lord of time, the Lord of His day, the Lord of all our lives. Jesus Christ has a reasonable claim on our time. The "Sabbath" is His gracious gift to recreate body and soul. Let us not profane this gift. Let us keep it a holy day, even though others all around us may turn it into a holiday. Let us make it a day of rest and worship and joy. Let us go to His house on His day to worship Him in spirit and in truth. When we do this, the question won't be, "Can I do this on the Lord's day without breaking the Law?" The question will be, "If I do this, will I miss a blessing?"

Remember: The fourth commandment does not say, "Thou shall not enjoy life on Sunday." Rather it says, "Thou shalt enjoy life by keeping the Sabbath holy."

5
DON'T FORGET DEAR OLE MOM AND DAD
"Honor Thy Mother And Thy Father" (Exodus 20:12)

Let us keep in mind that the first four commandments touch man's relationship to God, the last six commandments touch man's relationship to his fellowman. Now, it must be extremely significant that the first commandment that is dealing with a person's relationship with his fellowman has to do with the home. Are we not safe in saying that if a person is to live righteously toward his fellows, he will need to be trained in a righteous home?

The fifth commandment says: "Honor thy father and thy mother, that thy days may be long upon the land which the Lord thy God giveth thee" (Exodus 20:12).

MEANING OF THE FIFTH COMMANDMENT- The first word in the commandment is a duty God requires of children. "Honor thy father and mother." In the plan of God, children are the offspring of their parents. Also, in the plan of God, parents are to control, protect, sustain, and train their children. Our parents are God's representatives. They are for us in God's stead. "What God is to the adult, parents are to the child – lawgiver and lover, provider and controller."[10] Therefore the attitude which God requires of the child to the parent is identical in kind, though not in degree, with that which man owes toward God Himself. He is required to show obedience, reverence and love.

I. OBEDIENCE TO THE COMMANDMENT- How do children keep this commandment?

---

[10] G. Campbell Morgan, *The Ten Commandments*, Fleming H. Revel Company, New York, 1901, p. 53.

1. First, we honor our parents by obeying them. If a child is not yet of age to think, to plan, to assume full responsibilities of adulthood, he is to obey his parents without question. This obedience is absolutely necessary because an immature mind must be guided, or else the life will be wrecked. A disobedient child is headed for serious trouble, if not definite destruction (Colossians 3:20).

   In Ephesians 6:1, this commandment is repeated, "Children obey your parents in the Lord; for this is right." In our modern society, children have changed this verse. It now reads, "Parents, obey your children for this is right." The modern home is disintegrating because parents have forgotten to make their children obey at all costs (2 Timothy 3:1-2).

2. Second, we honor our parents by loving and reverencing them. It is often assumed that the fifth commandment is addressed to young folks only. Nothing can be further from the truth. Unquestionably, it is addressed to children first, for in the order of nature, children are always young first. But no one, however old, is ever released from the duties of this commandment.

   Notice, the commandment does not say merely "obey" your parents. It says, "honor" them. Honor embraces love and affection, gratitude and respect. Look how strong the Bible is on this matter of revering parents:
   a. Exodus 21:15, "And he that smiteth his father, or his mother, shall be surely put to death."
   b. Exodus 21:17, "And he that curseth his father, or his mother, shall surely be put to death."

3. Third, we honor our parents by caring for them in their time of need. One of the most serious struggles of our day is the decision of what to do with people when they become old and helpless. Heathen races put them out to die. Love is the theme of Christianity and the individual is forever precious, so we

cannot be guilty of such. In our day institutional care is often best for our parents. We do not break the fifth commandment under such circumstances, provided we monitor and visit them constantly.

The Psalmist said, "Cast me not off in the time of old age; forsake me not when my strength faileth" (Psalm 71:9). This is a plea that should melt the heart of every child with a needy, helpless mother or father.

In Jesus' day if a man wanted to be rid of the care of his aged parents, All that he had to do was to say, "It is Corban." This meant that his money was dedicated to religion, and that he would be free of any responsibility to his parents. Jesus condemned this practice in scorching language. Paul reiterates this feeling in 1 Timothy 5:8 when he says, "But if any provide not for his own, and specially for those of his own house, he hath denied the faith, and is worse than an infidel."

Sometimes the old folks become irritable and grouchy. It is still the children's duty to take care of them. "If we must carry them in our arms, we remember that they fed us with a spoon. If we must clothe them, we must remember that they clothed us. If we must provide for them, we must remember that they provided for us. Jesus on the cross provided for His mother and again set an example for us."[11]

II, OBLIGATION OF PARENTS TO CHILDREN – How do parents keep this commandment?

Let us not forget the fifth commandment is not only a law for children; it includes an ideal life for parents of the most binding and stringent nature. In brief, if parents are to be honored, they

---

[11] W. Hershel Ford, *Simple Sermons on the Ten Commandments*, Zondervan Publishing House, Grand Rapids, Michigan, 1956, p. 67.

must be honorable. They must discipline their children in love. Neither a father or mother can think right thoughts or direct their children in the right paths unless they are living a life in subjection to God. God must order the parents' ways if they are to order their children. "Children, obey your parents in the Lord…And, ye fathers, provoke not your children to wrath; but bring them up in the nurture and the admonition of the Lord" (Ephesians 6:1,4). Notice, the commandment to the children and parents is conditioned by the phrase "in the Lord" (Colossians 3:21).

1. Parents must live clean if they expect their children to live pure lives.
2. Parents must use wholesome language if they expect their children not to employ profanity.
3. Parents must have clean habits if they expect their children to have clean habits.
4. Parents must be truthful if they expect their children to be honest.
5. Parents must be separated from the world if they expect their children to leave the world.
6. Parents must pray if they expect their children to pray.
7. Parents must give of themselves and of their finances if they expect their children to give.
8. Parents must read the Bible if they expect their children to respect God's Word.
9. Parents must be sure that they are not professing one thing and living something else in front of the child, or else the child will detect it. You cannot "kid" the "kids."
10. Parents must accept Jesus Christ as Savior and Lord if they expect to lead their children to God.
11. Parents must be faithful to the Church of Jesus Christ, or else they cannot expect their children to attend.

III. THE OUTCOME OF OBEDIENCE – Finally, connected with this commandment is a promise. "Honor thy father and mother, which is the first commandment with promise" (Ephesians

6:2). What is the promise? "That thy days may be long upon the land which the Lord thy God giveth thee."

Originally, this was a promise to the nation of Israel. "It is a perfectly correct interpretation to put upon the commandment to make it mean length of national existence in Palestine for the Jews. A nation reverencing and honoring parents will be a nation of home building, a nation in which the essential virtues and integrities will have high rank."[12] Homes produce upright children; upright children become good citizens and citizens build the nation. God's blessings always rest upon a nation of character. "Righteousness exalted a nation; but sin is a reproach to any people" (Proverbs 14:34).

Without doubt, there is also a personal application of this promise; for in the majority of cases the honoring of parents results in the realization of habits.

---

[12] J.C. Massee, *The Gospel In the 10 Commandments*, The Higley Press, Butler, Indiana, p. 77.

6
TAMPERING WITH GOD'S MOST SACRED GIFT
"Thou Shalt Not Kill." (Exodus 20:13)

God is the author of life, and He alone has the prerogative to take life. "The Lord brings death and makes alive" (1 Samuel 2:6). Therefore when a person destroys the life of his fellows, he is striking at God's supreme prerogative. In Psalm 8:4, David asked, "What is man?" The Bible answers that man is created in the image of God, the crown of His creation. The value of all humankind is based on two tremendous truths:
1. God created man in His own image
2. Jesus Christ shed His precious blood to redeem him.

I. EXPLANATION OF THE SIXTH COMMANDMENT - This commandment forbids the intentional murder of human life. The commandment says "You will do no murder." It is possible to kill and yet not to murder. All murder is, of course, killing, but all killing is not murder. Killing is the unintentional taking of life; murder consists of the intentional taking of life. In the Old Testament, there were Cities of Refuge where an unintentional manslayer might go and find protection.

II. EXCEPTIONS TO THE SIXTH COMMANDMENT - The sixth commandment does not forbid:
A. Accidental manslaughter.
B. The killing of animals for food and clothing. Albert Schweitzer would not kill an animal. But his philosophy was more Hindu than Biblical. God said to Noah, "Every moving thing that liveth shall be meat for you" (Genesis 9:3).
C. Capital Punishment. The right of capital punishment belongs to the government, which is ordained of God, not to an individual (Romans 13:1-4). When the State executes a man in the electric chair for a capital offense, the person who pulls the

switch is not a murderer. Jesus did not condemn the principle of capital punishment, although He certainly would have condemned the injustices connected with it.
D. Self-Defense under certain circumstances. The law of Moses made provision for this (see Numbers 35:22-35).
E. A Just War. Just as the judge has a right to condemn the murderer or the policeman has the right to shoot an armed criminal breaking into a home, so a government has the right to become an instrument of justice to stop evil men and nations. However, Christ never gives us, under any circumstances, the right to hate our enemies (Matthew 5:44). If you opt for war, it must be done in agony of spirit and only as a last resort.

III. EXAMPLES OF VIOLATIONS OF THE SIXTH COMMANDMENT
A. Direct Murder:
- The willful murder of another person.
- Mob Murder – A person is a murderer if he joins a mob or lynching crew.
- Suicide – If God does not allow us to murder another, He certainly does not allow us to murder ourselves. Taking your life is a privilege which belongs only to God and no Christian can do it. I am not condemning those who commit suicide. God alone is their judge. I believe some suicides are saved. Doubtless, many have taken their lives while suffering from a form of insanity.
- Murder by proxy – paying someone else to commit murder for you.
- Abortion – Roe verses Wade stated that the law does not regard abortion as murder, but as a form of birth control. But let's not confuse the issue of abortion with birth control. As a Protestant, I believe it is right to plan our families and space children properly for the health of the mother. Birth control might be termed "conception control," since it prevents the beginning of human life. But such birth control should not be

confused with abortion because abortion is the destruction of human life after it has begun.
- Mercy Killing – If an unborn human being can be destroyed before birth, why not legalize the killing of old people who are no longer useful? Persons who cannot get well? Mentally defective babies at birth? You may think I am exaggerating. However less than six months after England passed a permissive abortion law, a law was introduced into the Parliament to legalize mercy killing. It was barely defeated.

B. Indirect Murder:
- Overeating – digging our graves with knives and forks.
- Destructive Habits – smoking, alcohol and drugs.
- Dispensers - of alcohol and drugs
- Drunken Driving or driving under the influence
- Shabby work for personal gain – Engineers who knowingly design a faulty structure or use cheap materials in order to benefit from the profits.
- Removal of stop signs – I know of an occasion when three boys, as a prank, removed a stop sign and four people were killed.
- The premature murder of parents – For example: A father had two sons who came home drunk at two o'clock in the morning. The father handed each of them a pistol and told them to go upstairs and kill their mother. Quickly sobered, they asked, "Why?" He replied, "It would be kinder for you to kill her with these pistols than to kill her by inches as you are doing with your behavior."

These are all forms of murder. Today more than ever, we must think about the vast implications of the sixth commandment.

IV. THE ELEVATION OF THE SIXTH COMMANDMENT –
The sixth commandment forbids the overt act of murder. But Jesus forbids not only murder, but the spirit which prompts it. "You have heard that it was said…You shalt not kill, and whosoever shall kill

shall be in danger of the judgment" (Matthew 5:21-22). Murder, as an attitude in the heart – anger, resentment, and hatred – is a part of our old natures. "Out of the heart proceed…murders," says Jesus in Mark 7:21. This is why every human being, including the good moral person, needs a new birth (John 3:3). There are many murderers walking the street, who never killed any person. Some murderers attend church every Sunday. You are a murderer, says the apostle John, when you hate your brother or cherish malice in your heart toward him. "Anyone who keeps on hating his brother is a murderer, and you know that no murderer can have eternal life remaining in him" (1 John 3:15, Williams Translation).

V. THE EXTRAORDINARY MURDER OF ALL HISTORY - This murder took place 1900 years ago – just outside the wall of old Jerusalem. The victim was the sinless, perfect, matchless Son of God. He was murdered on a cruel Roman cross. Who murdered Him? The song asks, "Were you there when they crucified my Lord?" You would say, "No, I wasn't there. I was not even born." Ah, but you and I were there. We were represented at the cross by our sins. The Roman soldiers and Jewish leaders were the instruments, but "He was wounded for my transgressions, He was bruised for my iniquities, the punishment which secured my peace was upon Him; and by His stripes I am healed" (Isaiah 53:5). Because of this glorious fact, I do not have to bear my sins. Jesus will forgive and cleanse me if I will admit I am a sinner and repent, after which He, through the Holy Spirit, will make me a new person (2 Corinthians 5:7). Love will then overflow my heart and instead of hating (even in my heart) and murdering my fellow human beings, I will "love my enemies, bless them that curse me, do good to them that hate me, and pray for them who despitefully use me and persecute me" (Matthew 5:44).

7
IT'S SEX O'CLOCK IN AMERICA
"Thou Shalt Not Commit Adultery." (Exodus 20:14)

In his book, <u>The Myth of the Greener Grass</u>, Allen Peterson tells the story of a woman who was at lunch with eleven friends. They had been studying French together while their children were in nursery school. One woman asked the group, "How many of you have been faithful to your husband throughout your marriage?" Only one woman raised her hand. That evening the woman told her husband the story and added that she had not raised her hand. "But I have been faithful," she assured him. "Then why didn't you raise your hand?" "I was ashamed." Ashamed of fidelity! In the past the shame fell on those who broke their vows, but in our society, "affairs" seem to be the modern, sophisticated thing to do. The media makes you believe that only killjoys still believe in fidelity. It is sex o'clock in America, yet God still says, "You will not commit sexual immorality."

I. THE SUBSTANCE OF THE SEVENTH COMMANDMENT.
Adultery is derived from the Latin root which means to adulterate, or weaken, corrupt and make impure. Adultery is the perversion of one of God's creative gifts into a destructive force. Adultery covers every sexual immorality on the part of married and unmarried: Adultery, Fornication, Incest, Homosexuality, Lesbianism, Oral Sex, Child Abuse, Pornography, Lust in the heart, Unmarried "live-ins," Bestiality (sex with animals), Necrophilia (sex with the dead), and Premarital Sex.

II. THE SCRIPTURAL PROHIBITIONS AND WARNINGS AGAINST SEXUAL IMMORALITY.
In the Old Testament death was decreed both for the adulterer and adulteress (Leviticus 20:10. The New Testament clearly states that the practicing adulterer cannot enter heaven (1 Corinthians 6:10;

Galatians 5:19; Revelation 21:8. But thank God the adulterer can be forgiven, if he repents and turns to Christ. Jesus commands that whatever entices you to immorality, turn from it, give it up, cut it off. The handicapped person with only one eye and hand is better off than the person who is whole but involved in immorality, says Jesus (Matthew 5:29-30). It is better to be sexually frustrated and lonely than to bear the scars of infidelity. The person who keeps himself pure retains his dignity and self-worth. More importantly, he keeps his fellowship with God. Jesus says in Matthew 5:8, "Blessed are the pure in heart: for they shall see God."

III. THE STATISTICS ON VIOLATION OF THE SEVENTH COMMANDMENT.

"America has become a sexual nuthouse" says novelist, John Osborn. The media tells us in a thousand ways "Thou shalt lust in thought, word and deed." Our comedians, televisions shows, movies and novels ridicule as abnormal the Christian faith's teaching of purity and sanctity. Marriage, chastity, commitment and self-control are derided and dismissed as ideas belonging to the "Dark Ages." The New York Times polled 100,000 woman and discovered: 80% had sex before marriage, 30% had extra-marital sex with two to five men after marriage, and 64% had sex with men other than their husbands.

IV. SOCIO-ECONOMIC-RELIGIO FORCES CONTRIBUTING TO IMMORALITY.

Just think of the alarming attack on sexual morality mounted by this adulterous generation. Sexual sins have always existed, but for the first time a "Playboy" philosophy of immorality has emerged in our culture, which says, "Sex is a function of the body, a drive we share with animals, like eating, drinking and sleeping. It is a physical demand which must be satisfied. If we don't satisfy it, the repression will cause all kinds of neuroses and psychoses. Let's forget the old ways. Throw away those inhibitions. Find a like-minded partner and let yourself go."

The saddest developments of all is that many sections of the church are wavering or actually teaching anti-biblical sexual ethics. For example, Bishop John Spong states, "Sex drove me to the Bible.. I was led to question traditional religious attitudes and traditional religious definitions on a wide variety of sexual issues, from homosexuality to premarital living..."[13] How relevant the words of Chaucer, "If gold rusts, what will iron do?"

V. THE SOLUTION TO THE SWEEPING IMMORALITY OF OUR DAY.

Jesus says that "Out of the heart proceed...adulteries and fornication..."(Matthew 15:19). This means the sexual problem is the problem of the human heart. The heart must be cleansed and changed. Only Jesus Christ can do this through His cleansing blood, and He can do it only if we turn to Him in repentance and sincere trust. Jesus delighted in restoring immoral people in His day (John 4 and John 8). He will forgive any person who turns to Him in genuine repentance. He will make you a new person (2 Corinthians 5:17) and give you the power to live a moral life. Pastor, writer, and premier youth leader in America, Josh McDowell discovered through a special survey that the "number one barrier to sexual immorality among youth was being born again."

You must have a personal relationship with Jesus Christ through the new birth. Ask yourself this question, "At some point in the past, did I realize that I was a lost sinner, did I turn from my sins (repent), and did I trust Jesus with all my heart, and is Jesus living within me today?" "If any person is in Christ, he is a new creation; behold, old things have passed away, and all things become new." (2 Cor. 5:17).

---

[13] John Shelby Spong, *Living in Sin? A Bishop Rethinks Human Sexuality*, Harper and Row, New York, 1988.

Even after you are born again, you must take every precaution against sexual temptation. Herewith are seven steps to victory which were lifted directly from the Scriptures:

1. Daily you must ask and permit the Holy Spirit to control your thoughts and actions. The Bible then promises that you will never fulfill the lusts of the flesh (sexual sins and other evils). Galatians 5:16 promises "Live your life under the control of the Holy Spirit and you will never satisfy the desires of your sinful nature." What a wonderful promise to young men and women!

2. Depend upon the triangle of help God has provided for you:
   a. The Bible – read regularly – "Thy Word have I hid in my heart, so I will not sin against God." (Psalm 119:11).
   b. Prayer – Jesus said, "People must always pray and not lose heart." (Luke 18:1).
   c. The Church – stay close to God's people. Their very presence will encourage you to live a clean life. "Forsake not the assembling of yourselves together" (in church, that is). (Hebrews 10:25).

3. Be sure that the people that you spend time with are clean, strong in faith, and committed to Jesus. My mother used to say, "If you lie down with dogs, you will get up with fleas." The Bible puts it this way, "Do not be mislead, bad company corrupts character." (1 Cor. 15:33).

4. If single, do not date any person who is not a Christian and an active Church member. (Proverbs 15:5)

5. Listen to those who love you when they caution you against some action or habit. "A fool despiseth his father's instruction" (Proverbs 15:5).

6. When tempted to sin, talk confidentially to someone you trust – your parents, grandparents, godly teacher, or pastor.

7. Be comforted in this, "No good thing will the Lord withhold from him or her who walks uprightly" (Psalm 84:11b).
- "Flee from sexual immorality" (1 Corinthians 6:18).
- "Watch your company" (1 Corinthians 15:33).
- "Watch what you see, read and think" (Job 31:1; Proverbs 23:7).
- "Saturate your life with God's Word" (Psalm 119:11).
- "Depend constantly upon the power of the Holy Spirit" (Galatians 5:16).
- "Stay close to the family of God" (Malachi 3:16; Hebrews 10:25).
- "Pray without ceasing" (1 Thessalonians 5:17).
- "Don't give the Devil a chance" (Ephesians 4:27).

WHAT DO I DO IF I HAVE ALREADY SINNED?
Listen, God knows all about you. He knows what you've done, what's been done to you, and the good news is that He still loves you. He is far more eager to forgive you than He is to judge you. Before He will forgive and cleanse, you must repent and turn to the Lord completely. When you do,… "though your sins be as scarlet, they shall be as white as snow." (Isaiah 1:18) As someone expressed it, you will be a "secondary virgin." Then be very careful not to fall back into the old lifestyle which caused you to sin.

The Bible teaches that the strongest person who ever lived was Samson. And what was his downfall? A relationship with the woman Delilah. The wisest person who ever lived was Solomon. And his downfall? He married foreign wives who turned his heart away from the Lord. The holiest person who ever lived was David. Twice the Bible calls him "a man after God's own heart." Yet an adulterous relationship with Bathsheba proved to be his downfall.

Now if the strongest, wisest and holiest persons who ever lived all struggle with their sexuality, do you think we today who aren't so strong, holy and wise might be struggling ourselves? And indeed, we are! But we don't have to yield. God has shown us a way out. "There is no temptation that has overtaken you except what is common to man, but God is faithful who will not suffer you to be tempted above what you are able but will also with the temptation make a way of escape that you may be able to bear it (1 Cor. 10:13). This way of escape is to cling to Jesus and by His power to live by His standards.

8
WHY THERE IS NO FREE LUNCH
"Thou Shalt Not Steal" (Exodus 20:15)

Religion is growing in popularity in America , says Mr. Gallup, but at the same time THEFT is strangely on the increase. Some good examples of this are people cheating on their income taxes and expense accounts. The eighth commandment clearly forbids stealing. The Hebrew has only three words, "Do Not Steal" which is pretty straightforward.

I. SCRIPTURAL BACKGROUND ON THE EIGHTH COMMANDMENT.

The Bible teaches that everything in existence belongs to God (Psalm 24:1), but God has given His creatures the things they need for life. So while man is on this earth, he has the God-given right of possession. To deny any person that right violates the very basis of God's creation which is why there is no free lunch. The Communist idea that property belongs to the State is a colossal lie and has proven disastrously unworkable where it has been tried.

II. SIMPLE DEFINITION OF STEALING

Stealing is taking from another person things entrusted to him by God and which he needs for life. Stealing is trying to get something for nothing at another's expense. Things which can be stolen are: Money, property, land, wife, children, dogs, livestock, freedom, faith, happiness, opportunity, reputation, time, position, et al. Stealing is getting the reward without paying the price; collecting the dividend without making the investment, receiving money without working, making good grades without studying, trying for the top of the ladder without climbing the rungs. The devil tried to get Jesus to take shortcuts (really steal His way) to gain advantage (Matthew 4) but Jesus knew there could be no crown without a cross, no redemption without a suffering Redeemer, and no resurrection without a crucifixion. All who would follow Jesus must live under this principle of the cross (Luke 9:23).

III. SIZES AND SHAPES OF STEALING IN AMERICAN CULTURE:
- RANK STEALING: Theft of: Money, autos, houses, land, inheritance, Books, tools, clothing, bicycles, watermelons, hubcaps, televisions, towels, jewelry.

- RATIONALIZED STEALING: Employer "ripping " off employee, employee "ripping" off employer, income tax evasion, padding expense accounts, cheating in sports, cheating on tests, price gouging, excessive charging and debt, taking home tools and office supplies, stealing one's education. Illustration: Some years ago the President of a great Southern University received a letter from a prominent businessman, who was one of the school's most famous graduates. In the letter he enclosed his A. B. degree diploma and wrote, "I am no longer keeping something which doesn't really belong to me. I cheated on my senior examinations and did not pass them fairly...I stole my college education."

- The WORST FORM OF "RATIONALIZED STEALING" IS GAMBLING. Remember stealing is basically trying to get something for nothing and at another's expense. This is exactly what gambling is. This is what the State Lottery is. "FBI crime reports have shown that states that allow gambling have a much higher crime rate than non-gambling states. The idea that a nation can raise money by gambling is a myth. For every dollar generated by gambling, several dollars are required in higher police, court, penitentiary and relief costs. Perfect illustrations of this are Reno and Las Vegas, Nevada where the police force is three times larger than in cities of comparable size."[14]

---

[14] David A. Seamands, God's Blueprint for Living, Bristol Books, Wilmore, Kentucky, 1988, p. 114.

Gambling not only violates not the eighth commandment but also the spirit of the whole New Testament because it substitutes chance and fate for the fatherly care of a loving God. I personally believe that gambling is a form of stealing, including the lottery. For this reason I oppose a lottery for the great state of North Carolina.

- RESPECTABLE STEALING: Stealing one's liberty, opportunity, morality, time, advantage, faith, or destroying one's reputation. <u>Illustration</u>: Shakespeare put his finger on the worst form of stealing when he told us, "He that filches from me my good name robs me of that which not enriches him and makes me poor indeed." Illustration: When Mark Twain married Olivia Langdon she was a very devout Christian. He was so critical of her faith that she gave it up. Later, there came into her life a very deep sorrow. He urged, "Livy, lean on your faith." Sadly she told him, "I can't. I haven't any left." To his dying day he was haunted by the fact that he had stolen from his wife her most valuable treasure.

IV STEALING FROM GOD – There are several ways that people are stealing from God. Listed below are a few examples:
A. Robbing God of His credibility by shabby living (Romans 2:24).
B. Refusing to give God the time and talent due Him (Romans 12:1-2).
C. Refusing to pay tithes and offerings (Matthew 3:8-10; Luke 6:38; 2 Corinthians 9:6-8; 1 Corinthians 16:2).

V. SOLUTION FOR STEALING:
A. Get Jesus in your heart.
B. Practice laboring rather than loafing (Ephesians 4;28).
C. Live to give rather than to get (Acts 20:35).
D. Love your fellow humans rather than leech them. "Love seeketh not its own" (1 Corinthians 13:5).
E. Restore stolen things if possible (Luke 19:8).

CONCLUSION: Once Jesus told a story of a man who was taking a journey from Jerusalem to Jericho. He fell among thieves, who robbed and beat him and left him half dead on the roadside. A Samaritan came along, helped the man, and provided financial provision for his convalescence (Luke 10:30-37). In that graphic story we have three philosophies of wealth:

1. THE THIEF - "What is thine is mine – I'll take it."
2. PRIEST AND LEVITES – "What is mine is mine – I'll keep it."
3. GOOD SAMARITAN – "What is mine is thine – I'll share it."

The last philosophy is the way of Jesus. Which way will you follow?

9
HUNG BY THE TONGUE
"Thou Shalt Not Bear False Witness" (Exodus 20:16)

TONGUE SCRIPTURES:
- Psalm 19:14; Psalm 141:3; Proverbs 10:11; Proverbs 16:24
- Proverbs 25:11; Psalm 120:2; Matthew 12:37;
- Ephesians 4:25; James 3

The favorite indoor sport of Americans is talking about their neighbors, and much of this talking is plain lying. You can convince anyone he is a sinner by asking one question, "Did you ever tell a lie?" Anyone who is honest will say yes. Thus the Ninth Commandment should sound loudly into each of our ears.

I. THE SUBSTANCE OF THE NINTH COMMANDMENT - The commandment in its original form probably concerned the simple legal matter of not lying about ones neighbor in a court of law. But the prophets and later Jesus expanded this commandment to forbid every form of lying. These will be discussed under point IV.

II. THE SOURCE OF LYING – Jesus said in John 8:44 that "the Devil is a 'liar' and also the father of lies." Satan beguiled Eve in the garden by a lie (Genesis 3:4). Adam became a deceiver the day he sinned, and he passed the tendency to deceive, cover-up, pretend and to lie, to all human beings.

"One reason we break this commandment is because it ministers to our own pride. It takes some of the sting out of our own failures if we can rub off the glitter of someone else's crown. It is a sign of an inferiority complex when a person tells of the faults of another. Back of much gossip is jealousy. However, hardly anybody feels guilt for violating this law. I have had people confess to me the breaking of every one of the Ten Commandments except this one. I have never heard a person admit to gossiping. We say, "I don't mean to talk about him but..." and off we go. We assume a self-righteous attitude which we feel gives us license to condemn sin. But all the time we enjoy talking about the sin and, in a backhanded way, brag of ourselves because we have not done exactly what the person we are telling about has done. Sometimes our gossip takes the form of a false sympathy. "Isn't it too bad how Mr. Blank beats his wife? I am so sorry for her." Or maybe we just ask a question. "Is it true that Mr. and Mrs. Blank are on the verge of a divorce?" That is the method of the devil. He would not accuse Job of wrongdoing. Instead, he merely asked, "Doth Job fear God for nought?" (Job 1:9). The mere question raises a suspicion as to Job's sincerity."[15]

III. THE SERIOUSNESS OF LYING – Lying is serious business because:
1. Lying destroys human relationships. Harmonious relationships are based on trust and there can be no trust where there is lying (Ephesians 4:25).
2. Lying demeans character.
3. Lying destroys lives. Jesus lost his life at Calvary because the people lied on him (Matthew 26:59-61).
4. Lying dethrones God. God is truth and he cannot lie (Titus 1:2), and he hates a "false witness that speaketh lies" (Proverbs 16:9).
5. Lying damns the soul.

IV. THE SHAPES AND SIZES OF LYING. – The Ninth Commandment and its restatement in the New Testament forbids lying in the following ways:

---

[15] Charles L. Allen, *The Ten Commandments, An Interpretation*, Fleming H. Revell Company, Westwood, New Jersey, 1965, pp. 54-55.

A. <u>Speaking a lie</u>　　　<u>Example:</u>
　　Direct Lying　　　　False Witness in Court
　　Judging　　　　　　Innuendos
　　Flattery　　　　　　Half Truths
　　Criticism　　　　　Truth out of Context
　　Fault Finding　　　False Political Promises
　　Silence　　　　　　Certain Questions

"When someone praises someone else we, like Satan, say, 'Sure. He's good, but look what he's getting out of it. What do you think he's doing it for?' For example, when a person is successful and someone says, 'Boy, her career has really taken off,' we say, 'Yeah, but how do you think she got where she is?' That's all we say. We just sow that doubt. When a woman is popular and has a lot of dates and someone says, 'Guys really like her, don't they?' We agree. Then we deliver the punch line, or rather the line that punches a hole in her character. We say, 'Sure, men hang around her. But you know why, don't you?' And that's all it takes."[16]

B. Spreading Lies
　1. Gossip
　2. Slander
　3. Tale Bearing (Leviticus 19:16; 1 Timothy 5:13).

C. Teaching or preaching a lie.

D. Singing a lie – "I surrender all"

E. Writing a lie. Example: False advertising, Communist Manifesto, Humanist Manifesto #2.

---

[16] Semands, p. 127.

F. Promising a lie. Example: The Marriage Vows- In this day and time, marriage vows are flippantly made. The attitude is, if it doesn't work out, there is always divorce.

G. Living a lie – "1 John 1:6 says, 'If we claim to have fellowship with Him yet walk in the darkness, we lie and do not live by the truth.' You see, a lie is something that can be said, spread or lived. One can do a lie as well as speak and spread a lie. The living lie is the lie of deceiving ourselves. When what we witness to loudly and clearly with our lips is proven false by our life, we are living a lie. The road Jesus took to the cross was lived with this kind of living liar: the scribes who claimed to have knowledge they didn't possess; the Pharisees who claimed to be righteous but were not; the false witnesses who told stories of things they had not seen or heard; Judas, whose loving gesture, a kiss, was the very incarnation of a living lie; and Pilate, who sounded so sincere and pious at the trial when he asked, 'What is truth?' to disguise his cowardly, lying heart. You see, the greatest lies of all are the lies we tell ourselves about ourselves. We don't tell these lies for profit or to destroy anyone else but for the sake of our own pride. The biggest lie is when we attempt to maintain a false image of ourselves as sinless and not in need of salvation."[17]

H. Lying to God – A good example of this would be Ananias and Sapphira in Acts 5.

THE BIGGEST LIE OF THE 20TH CENTURY IS COMMUNISM. THE BIGGEST LIE IN AMERICA IS SECULAR HUMANISM. THE BIGGEST ULTIMATE LIAR WILL BE THE ANIT-CHRIST.

---

[17] Semands, p. 128.

V. THE SOLUTION TO LYING - Human beings do not have to be taught to lie. It is instinctive to the unregenerate person. Even children lie. Why? Jesus told the Pharisees that they spoke lies because their hearts were evil. "Out of the abundance of the heart the mouth speakth" (Matthew 12:34). So the heart of our lying problem is the problem of the heart. We read in Jeremiah 17:9, "The heart is deceitful above all things, and desperately wicked: who can know it?" Thus the solution for a lying tongue is a new heart. This is the reason every person needs a new nature through the new birth. Jesus Christ came to make us new creations in Him. When you truly repent and permit Jesus to take control of your life, then you have truth in the "inner parts" (Psalm 51:6). Then you will love truth, hate lying, and speak the truth.

As we stand before the cross we realize the truth is that we are bad enough to crucify the Son of God. That's the truth of the human heart. God has known that truth a long time, and perhaps now you know it too. Admit it and confess it to Him. The moment you do, the power of the lie, the hold of darkness and untruth, is broken.

When we confess and repent of our lies, His Holy Spirit, the Spirit of truth, begins a miracle in our lives, leading us from lying and darkness to truthfulness and light. As Will Rogers said, "So live that you would not be ashamed to sell the family parrot to the gown gossip."

There is so much bad in the best of us,
And so much good in the worst of us,
That it hardly behooves any of us,
To talk about the rest of us.

10
A "RESPECTABLE" BUT DEVASTATING SIN
"Thou Shalt Not Covet" (Exodus 20:17).

"Thou shalt not covet thy neighbor's house, thou shalt not covet thy neighbor's wife, nor his manservant, nor his maidservant, nor his ox nor his ass, nor any thing that is thy neighbor's" (Exodus 20:17).

The tenth commandment differs noticeably from those which precede it in that it deals with the inner motives of the heart. It is possible to violate this commandment and never be exposed to our fellowmen.

MEANING OF THE TENTH COMMANDMENT. – The word "covet" means to have an inordinate desire to possess. We covet when we set our hearts upon something, especially that which belongs to another. We covet when we allow our wants to rule over us.

Specifically, the commandment says:
1. You are not to covet your neighbor's house. This means that you are not to desire his real estate or property, such as buildings, lands, fish ponds, etc.
2. You are not to covet your neighbor's servants. Some folk have servants or employees working for them. It is coveting to try to steal them away from their employer.
3. You are not to covet your neighbor's ass or ox. This means that you are not to desire any of his personal property, such as pets, automobile, television, or even clothing.
4. You are not to covet your neighbor's wife. Vile-hearted people often seek to take another's wife or husband. This leads to tragedy, heartbreak and moral scandal.

The commandment ends saying, "You are not to covet anything that belongs to thy neighbor." This covers the whole field of human desire.

I. THE CHARACTERISTICS OF THE COVETEOUS PERSON.

1. A covetous person is one whose entire conception of value is materialistic. He gives all his time, thought, and attention to material things. He spends his life in pursuit of the things of the flesh. This man never reads God's Word, never takes time to pray, goes to church only for social reasons, and he never faces the fact that he must meet God someday in the judgment. He may be a man of many fine qualities. But his worldly pursuits close out God, and Jesus, and eternal life and Heaven. As Paul declares, he is an "idolater" (Ephesians 5:5). He may not worship a graven image, but in his heart he worships some material object. Every unregenerate person, to some extent, is a covetous person. His value is of this world.

2. A covetous person will exchange his soul for material things. One day a fine man who was immensely wealthy, but hungry in heart came to Jesus. Jesus in effect, said to this young man, "Young man, you must make a choice. You are in love with money, yet you need to be saved. You must choose between Me and your money." Jesus was telling the young man that he must transfer his affections from the material to the spiritual, from the world to God. The young man turned away from Jesus sorrowfully, for he had great possessions (Matthew 19). He was going to cling to his possessions if it cost him his soul. "What shall it profit a man if he gain the whole world and lose his soul?" (Matthew 16:26).

Multitudes of people covet the fleeting goods of this world more than the riches of eternity. Most of them will have their share of material things, but they will miss heaven and be lost forever without any riches. I know of no more disgusting person than one who is covetous. "It is a common saying, that a hog is good for nothing while he is alive. You cannot ride him like the horse; you cannot use him to draw like the ox; he does not provide clothing like the sheep; nor milk like the cow; he will not guard the house like a dog. He is good only for the slaughter. Like the hog, a covetous man is of little worth while he lives, for he does no good with his possessions. When he is dead, his goods are disposed of, and he uses them no more for his wallowing in the mire of sin."[18]

II. THE CURSE OF A COVETOUS SPIRIT - Coveting is one of the most perilous attitudes one can possess. A covetous spirit will cause you to break the other 9 commandments.

1. The first commandment tells us not to have other gods before the true God. A covetous person bows down before the god of materialism.

2. The second commandment tells us that we are not to make any graven images and bow down before them. A covetous person may not bow down before wooden or stone gods, but his heart bows in adoration before his material possessions.

3. The third commandment tells us not to take God's name in vain. We think of Ananias and Sapphira, who coveted money and who lied in the name of God and broke this commandment.

4. The fourth commandment tells us to keep the Sabbath day holy. God's day is broken more because of covetousness than for any other reason.

5. The fifth commandment tells us to honor our father and mother. A man who loves money will dishonor his parents in

---

[18] Lehman Strauss, *The Eleven Commandments*, Loizeaux Brothers, Inc. Publishers, New York, 1955, p. 153.

making it. He may refuse provision for them in order to store up for himself.

6. The sixth commandment tells us not to kill. A covetous heart has but one step to take before he is a murderer.
   a. David coveted Uriah's wife, and had him killed.
   b. Judas coveted money and betrayed the innocent Savior into the enemy's hands to be murdered – for only the price of one slave.
   c. The newspapers carry many accounts of murder, the real reason being that the heirs want to collect on the property that is left.

7. The seventh commandment tells us not to commit adultery. Prostitution is one of the oldest professions in the world. It is done for money. David coveted his neighbor's wife and committed adultery with her.

8. The eighth commandment tells us not to steal. But nearly all stealing is caused by covetousness, an insatiable desire for material things.

9. The ninth commandment tells us not to lie. But a truly covetous man can generally be bought with a price. He says, "If you pay me enough, I will go on the witness stand and tell what will benefit you." The covetous man will make money and acquire property by "hook or crook."

III. THE CURE FOR COVETING. Coveting is part of the old nature (Colossians 3:5; Romans 1:29). A person must receive a new nature through the new birth in order to have the power to overcome this natural tendency. With Christ enthroned in your heart you have the power to turn coveting into a positive force in your life.

1. Unlawful coveting may be counteracted by lawful coveting. For instance, Paul commands us: "Covet earnestly the best gifts" (1 Corinthians 13:31). It is right for a Christian to desire to cultivate his gifts and to improve his usefulness for the Lord, provided he is not motivated by selfish interest.

2. Coveting may be cured by contentment. A Christian's sufficiency is in Christ. Paul knew this and wrote, "I have learned in whatsoever state I am, therewith to be content" (Philippians 4:11). Paul had not always had this spirit, but circumstances had taught Paul to trust Christ for all things. "But godliness with contentment is great gain" (1 Timothy 6:6).

3. Coveting may be cured by complete trust in God. We covet when we become over anxious for material things. Paul commands in Philippians 4:6, "Be careful for nothing but in everything by prayer and supplication with thanksgiving let your request be made known unto God." Let us pray with David, "Incline my heart unto Thy testimonies, and not to covetousness" (Psalm 119:36).

11
CAN A CHRISTIAN KEEP THE TEN COMMANDMENTS?

In our discussion of the commandments thus far, we have sought to do two things:
1. to explain the meaning of each commandment, and
2. to show how the commandment applies to our lives.

But the question remains, how can individual Christians actually obey, or live out the commandments? The answer is found in the greatest commandment of all. When Jesus was asked, by a lawyer, "Which is the greatest commandment in the law," He replied, "Thou shalt love the Lord your God with all thy heart, and with all thy soul, and with all thy mind. This is the first and greatest commandment. And the second is like unto it, Thou shalt love thy neighbor as thyself. On these two commandments hang all the law and the prophets" (Matthew 22:37-40).

"Interestingly, it was a lawyer who quizzed Jesus about the law. Lawyers spend much of their time asking questions in order to test people –that's their job. And that was the job of the New Testament scribes, the Jewish religious lawyers of their time.

By Jesus' day the Jews had 611 different commandments: 365 negative ones and 246 positive ones. A religious life had become a terrible burden to the sincere person who really wanted to please God. Competent lawyers were needed to keep track of all the commandments and to interpret them properly. So the question Jesus was asked was not really a trick question. Determining the greatest commandment was an issue that generated a great deal of controversy and debate in that day."[19]

---

[19] Semands, p. 9.

The key, then, to obeying the Ten Commandments is "love." But what is "love" as stated in the command of Jesus? It is a special kind of love, agape love, one of several words for love in the Greek language. In English we use the word love in many different contexts. "I love chocolate ice cream. I love basketball. I love a good book. I love my wife and children. Under our word "love" we lump these and other good, healthy loves with the many kinds of sordid relationships that exist between people today. But agape love is a principle by which we can order our lives. It is first and foremost not an emotion but a quality of the will, a commitment of the total person, an arranging of our lives' priorities. Agape love can be demonstrated but not defined. God so loved that he gave (see John 3:16).

Agape love does include our emotions, but it is just as real when we do not have conscious thoughts of fellowship. A person who has agape love is directed toward, surrendered to and living for God. So biblically speaking, love is more closely related to the will than to the emotions."[20]

God alone is the source of agape love. Other loves, expressed in other Greek words, are natural to human beings and there is nothing wrong with them, but they cannot fulfill the greatest commandment given by Jesus. Eros love is physical or sexual love. Storge love is family affection. Philio love is warm personal friendship.

"So the real question boils down to this: how can I get this kind of agape love in my heart? Do I grit my teeth and say "I will love Jesus, I will love my neighbor, I will love them, even if it kills me? If this is my attitude, it probably will kill me. It will certainly kill agape love."[21]

---

[20] *Ibid.* p. 12.
[21] *Ibid.* p. 13.

The Bible seeks to encapsulate the meaning of agape love in five statements:

1. Agape love begins with God. "This is love, not that we loved God, but God loved us and sent His Son as the atoning sacrifice for our sins" (1 John 4:10). "We love God because He first loved us" ((1 John 4:19).

2. Agape love is demonstrated at the cross. "When we look at the cross we see something unlike anything else in all the world. We see that at the very place we hurt God the most, where we must have looked the worst to God, that's the place where God loved us the most. Isn't that a miracle? Isn't that wonderful?"[22]

3. Agape love is experienced in our hearts by repentance and faith. This means agape love is available to those who are surrendered and loving God.

4. Agape love comes into our hearts as a response to God's agape love for us. "Only love can beget love, only agape from God can reproduce it in our hearts. Love comes when we believe that we are loved and forgiven. Love comes when we accept the fact that we are accepted."[23]

5. Agape love matures as we surrender to the Holy Spirit. "The love of God is being poured out in our hearts by the Holy Spirit whom He has given us" (Romans 5:5). "The righteous requirements of the law is fulfilled in us who walk not after the flesh but after the Spirit" (Romans 8:4).

The question, then, to ask yourself is this: Am I obeying the greatest commandment? "On what level of life am I living? The lowest level is instinct, where we are driven by fleshly desires and urges. The next level is law, mere outward obedience and conformity with no

---

[22] *Ibid.* p. 14.
[23] *Ibid.* p. 13.

inward change. For people living at this level (and the number is legion)*, religion is a duty and often a great drudgery. The third level is a mixture of law and love, a life of duty with occasional flashes of love and devotion. People at this level may be outwardly obedient but experience little enjoyment."[24]

But thank God there is a higher, spiritual level to which God calls us and in which He enables us to abide: When love becomes the law of our lives, duty then becomes devotion and indescribable joy. God both enables us to love Him and to delight in that love. "Faithful is He who has called us, who also will do it" (1 Thess. 5:25). If we allow God, He will move into our hearts and give us the power to live up to the greatest commandment of all, and in so doing we will be enabled to obey the ten commandments.

---

*writer's words
[24] *Ibid.* p. 16.

www.ingramcontent.com/pod-product-compliance
Lightning Source LLC
LaVergne TN
LVHW051156080426
835508LV00021B/2653